# Jumpstarters for Analogies

## Short Daily Warm-ups for the Classroom

BY
LINDA ARMSTRONG

COPYRIGHT © 2010 Mark Twain Media, Inc.

ISBN 978-1-58037-533-7

Printing No. CD-404130

Mark Twain Media, Inc., Publishers
Distributed by Carson-Dellosa Publishing LLC

Visit us at www.carsondellosa.com

# Table of Contents

# Introduction to the Teacher

To succeed in today's competitive environment, students must improve their thinking skills. Quality classroom instruction remains the cornerstone of any instructional program, but experienced teachers know all learning requires reinforcement.

This book offers teachers and parents short warm-up activities to help young thinkers practice their craft. Used at the beginning of a language arts, science, spelling, geography, math, or health time slot, these mini-tasks help students focus on thinking and problem-solving skills.

The pages are grouped into units covering topics such as vocabulary, phonics, literature, science, geography, health, art and music, and math. Each page features five mini-activities.

Several types of analogies commonly appear on tests, and they are used here within the subject contexts. These include the following: part to whole (finger to hand), object to class (apple to fruit), object to action (dog to bark), synonym (little to small), antonym (little to big), sequence (first to second), and object to description (banana to yellow). These types are introduced in the first set of exercises.

> Before distributing the exercises, explain to students that colons (:) are used in a special way in analogies. For example, "big is to large as little is to small" is written big : large :: little : small.

There are many ways to use this book.

- Reproduce the pages, cut along the lines, and use each section as a ten-minute warm-up or part of a homework assignment.

- Distribute copies of uncut pages so students can keep their completed exercises in a three-ring binder for reference.

- For use at a learning center, reproduce each page, cut the exercises apart, and mount each on a card with the corresponding answer key section on the back. Laminate for durability.

- Make transparencies or Powerpoint slides for group lessons

**Note:** Share the exercises in any order that fits your ongoing program.

# Analogies Warm-ups:
# Solving Analogies: Related Pairs

---

Name/Date _____

## Solving Analogies: Related Pairs 1

How is each pair of words related? Circle the best description.

1. big : little        synonyms        antonyms        homophones
2. finger : hand    part/whole      object/description   object/use
3. morning : noon   object/use       object/description   sequence (order)
4. fall : break      cause/effect     object/kind        object/place
5. scissors : cut    person/action    object/action      whole/part

---

Name/Date _____

## Solving Analogies: Related Pairs 2

Match each word pair to the correct relationship.

1. tall : short       a. object/class
2. apple : fruit      b. object/action
3. small : little     c. antonyms
4. banana : yellow  d. synonyms
5. brush : paint     e. object/description

---

Name/Date _____

## Solving Analogies: Related Pairs 3

Use the clue to fill in the missing letters in the second word in each pair.

person/action    1. teacher : t _ _ _ hi _ g
person/object    2. teacher : m _ _ ke _
object/action    3. marker : ma _ _
degree          4. small : t _ _ y
member/group    5. fish : sc _ _ _ l

---

Name/Date _____

## Solving Analogies: Related Pairs 4

Use the clue to fill in the correct word.

| acting   sentence   fry   sixth   laugh |

cause/effect      1. joke : _____
part/whole        2. word : _____
person/action     3. actor : _____
sequence          4. fifth : _____
object/use        5. pan : _____

---

Name/Date _____

## Solving Analogies: Related Pairs 5

Use the clue to unscramble the second word in each pair.

synonyms        1. slender : htni    _____
antonyms        2. tiny : gheu       _____
sequence        3. one : wot         _____
whole/part       4. house : lwal      _____
object/class     5. snake : peerlit   _____

---

# Analogies Warm-ups:
# Vocabulary Analogies: Object/Characteristic

Name/Date _____

## Vocabulary: Object/Characteristic 1

Circle the best choice to complete the analogy.

1. banana : yellow :: plum :
   white        purple        pink

2. apple : red :: lemon :
   yellow        purple        blue

3. grapes : purple :: cantelope :
   blue        red            orange

4. lime : green :: cherry :
   green        red            blue

Name/Date _____

## Vocabulary: Object/Characteristic 2

Fill in the missing letters.

1. cactus : spiny :: rose : _ _ _ _ n _

2. glass : clear :: wood : o _ _ q _ e

3. velvet : soft :: steel : h _ _ _

4. sandpaper : rough :: foil : sm _ _ _ _

5. feather : light :: lead : h _ _ _ y

Name/Date _____

## Vocabulary: Object/Characteristic 3

Using the first part of the analogy as a clue, unscramble the last word in each analogy.

1. beach : warm :: mountains : _____        ocol

2. poles : icy :: equator : _____        tho

3. cottonball : fluffy :: marble : _____        nysih

4. cream : smooth :: apple : _____        rcpsi

5. night : dark :: day : _____        glhit

Name/Date _____

## Vocabulary: Object/Characteristic 4

Fill in the missing word.

| strong | hot | cold | cool | liquid |
|--------|-----|------|------|--------|

1. ice : solid :: water : _____

2. fire : hot :: ice : _____

3. breeze : gentle :: wind : _____

4. blanket : warm :: fan : _____

5. arctic : cold :: tropics : _____

Name/Date _____

## Vocabulary: Object/Characteristic 5

Match each word to the correct analogy.

1. lemon : sour :: candy : ____        a. sour

2. sugar : sweet :: fries : ____        b. spicy

3. chips : salty :: chili : ____        c. fruity

4. juice : fruity :: lime : ____        d. salty

5. salsa : spicy :: plum : ____        e. sweet

# Analogies Warm-ups: Vocabulary Analogies: Member/Group

Name/Date _____

## Vocabulary: Member/Group 1

Circle the best choice to complete the analogy.

1. student : class :: teacher :       pride       herd       faculty
2. fish : school :: person :          crowd       collection  constellation
3. card : deck :: star :              school      galaxy      corps
4. mountain : range :: wolf :         pack        troop       swarm
5. lion : pride :: sailor :           herd        den         crew

---

Name/Date _____

## Vocabulary: Member/Group 2

| senate | team | audience |
|--------|------|----------|
| colony | collection | |

Fill in the correct word.

1. cookie : batch :: coin : _____
2. member : club :: senator : _____
3. grape : bunch :: ant : _____
4. bee : swarm :: listener : _____
5. employee : staff :: player : _____

Name/Date _____

## Vocabulary: Member/Group 3

Match each word to the correct analogy.
1. dish : set :: whale : _____
2. stamp : collection :: kangaroo : _____
3. ship : fleet :: bird : _____
4. sheep : flock :: cow : _____
5. horse : herd :: rabbit : _____

a. mob   b. warren   c. pod
d. herd   e. flock

---

Name/Date _____

## Vocabulary: Member/Group 4

On your own paper, write each analogy in words. (Example: sheep : flock :: horse : herd is written as "sheep is to flock as horse is to herd")

1. tree : grove :: flower : bed
2. actor : cast :: singer : chorus
3. chapter : book :: room : building
4. block : neighborhood :: neighborhood : city

Name/Date _____

## Vocabulary: Member/Group 5

Fill in the blanks to complete the analogy.

1. cheerleader : squad :: musician : b _ _ d
2. firefighter : company :: athlete : t _ _ _
3. computer : network :: book : l _ _ r _ ry
4. kitten : litter :: buffalo : h _ _ d
5. tree : orchard :: vine : v _ _ _ y _ _ d

---

# Analogies Warm-ups: Vocabulary Analogies: Object/Action

Name/Date _____

## Vocabulary: Object/Action 1

Fill in the correct word from the choices in the box.

1. teeth : chew :: nose : _____
2. smoke : billow :: water : _____
3. grasshopper : hop :: mosquito : _____
4. clock : tick :: door : _____
5. snow : drift :: hail : _____

| creak |
| flow |
| pelt |
| sniff |
| fly |

Name/Date _____

## Vocabulary: Object/Action 2

Draw a line to match each word to the correct analogy.

1. bubble : drift :: ball :        swim
2. balloon : rise :: anchor :      honk
3. bee : sting :: skunk :          sink
4. frog : hop :: fish :            spray
5. duck : quack :: goose :         bounce

Name/Date _____

## Vocabulary: Object/Action 3

Fill in the missing letters to complete each analogy.

1. bird : sing :: frog : cr _ _ k
2. donkey : bray :: horse : _ e _ _ h
3. horse : trot :: duck : w _ _ _ l _
4. phone : ring :: horn : _ o _ _
5. knife : slice :: fork : pi _ _ _ e

Name/Date _____

## Vocabulary: Object/Action 4

Use the clue to unscramble the last word in each analogy.

1. glass : shatter :: rubber : _____ cebonu
2. top : spin :: skate : _____ olrl
3. snake : slither :: toad : _____ hpo
4. cat : pounce :: dog : _____ ubnod
5. wind : blow :: rain : _____ alfl

Name/Date _____

_____

## Vocabulary: Object/Action 5

Circle the best choice to complete the analogy.

1. finger : touch :: eye :

   hear    feel    watch

2. bell : toll :: horn :

   toot    ring    scream

3. lightning : flash :: thunder :

   ring    sing    rumble

4. scissors : cut :: spoon :

   cut    stir    paste

5. leaves : shake :: waves :

   ocean    water    break

# Analogies Warm-ups: Vocabulary Analogies: Part/Whole

---

Name/Date _____

## Vocabulary: Part/Whole 1

Circle the best choice.

1. tine : fork :: blade :      spoon   knife
2. bristle : brush :: tread :      tire   car
3. sleeve : shirt :: buckle :      hat   belt
4. sole : shoe :: crystal :      watch   table
5. key : piano :: string :      guitar   flute

---

Name/Date _____

## Vocabulary: Part/Whole 2

| roof   music   cabinet   branch   compass |

Fill in the best word.

1. hand : clock :: needle : _____
2. pixel : image :: note : _____
3. needle : bough :: leaf : _____
4. glass : window :: shingle : _____
5. drawer : dresser :: door : _____

---

Name/Date _____

## Vocabulary: Part/Whole 3

Match each word to the correct analogy.

1. sidewalk : street :: shoulder : _____
2. fingers : hand :: toes : _____
3. brim : cap :: heel : _____
4. nose : face :: hair : _____
5. elbow : arm :: knee : _____

a. leg
b. shoe
c. head
d. foot
e. highway

---

Name/Date _____

## Vocabulary: Part/Whole 4

Fill in the missing letters.

1. page : book :: shelf : li _ _ a _ y
2. nostril : nose :: lip : m _ _ t _
3. floor : room :: field : s _ _ d _ _ m
4. toe : sock :: finger : g _ _ v _
5. cover : book :: lid : b _ _

---

Name/Date _____

## Vocabulary: Part/Whole 5

On your own paper, write each analogy in words. (Example: drawer : dresser :: shelf : bookcase is written as "drawer is to dresser as shelf is to bookcase")

1. frame : picture :: fence : yard
2. knob : drawer :: handle : door
3. piece : puzzle :: letter : word
4. mattress : bed :: burner : stove
5. inch : foot :: foot : mile

---

# Analogies Warm-ups:
# Vocabulary Analogies: Object/Purpose

Name/Date _____

_____

## Vocabulary: Object/Purpose 1

Circle the best choice to complete the analogy.

1. shovel : dig :: box :

     write    eat    contain

2. pail : fill :: shirt :

     run    wear    sing

3. broom : sweep :: tack

     drink    believe    hold

4. chair : sit :: nose :

     hear    smell    see

5. lamp : illuminate :: ear :

     see    hear    taste

Name/Date _____

## Vocabulary: Object/Purpose 2

Fill in the missing word from the choices in the box.

1. scissors : cut :: needle : _____
2. ruler : measure :: file : _____
3. fork : eat :: printer : _____
4. staple : fasten :: toothbrush : _____
5. glue : stick :: calculator : _____

| clean |
| smooth |
| add |
| print |
| sew |

Name/Date _____

## Vocabulary: Object/Purpose 3

Circle "T" for true or "F" for false about each analogy.

1. pen : write :: envelope : enclose     T   F
2. pan : cook :: soap : slice            T   F
3. towel : dry :: television : write     T   F
4. water : drink :: flashlight : light   T   F
5. food : eat :: marker : mark           T   F

Name/Date _____

## Vocabulary: Object/Purpose 4

Fill in the missing letters.

1. eraser : erase :: detergent : _ _ s _
2. marker : mark :: car : d _ i _ _
3. pencil : write :: food : _ _ t
4. book : read :: platter : s _ _ v _
5. money : pay :: fan : c _ _ _

Name/Date _____

## Vocabulary: Object/Purpose 5

Use the clue to unscramble the last word in each analogy.

1. pool : swim :: bed : _____     lsepe
2. brush : paint :: mop : _____   elnac
3. crayon : color :: cup : _____  rdkni
4. glasses : see :: headphones : _____   lstnie
5. camera : photograph :: dryer : _____   yrd

# Analogies Warm-ups:
# Vocabulary Analogies: Synonyms and Antonyms

Name/Date _____

## Vocabulary: Synonyms and Antonyms 1

Circle the synonym that best completes the analogy.

1. total : sum :: flat :        hilly  level
2. purpose : goal :: great :    ordinary  grand
3. fury : rage :: happy :       glad  miserable
4. answer : reply :: exclaim :    declare  ask
5. begin : start :: halt :        stop  run

Name/Date _____

## Vocabulary: Synonyms and Antonyms 2

Underline the missing antonym that completes the analogy.

1. love : hate :: like :   erlmdislikekjwer
2. entertain : bore :: play :  qazxworkatwb
3. boy : girl :: man :  fdeascwomanmoutr
4. husband : wife :: father :   opeymothercixzon
5. open : close :: give :  kuewnvtakewetupm

Name/Date _____

## Vocabulary: Synonyms and Antonyms 3

Fill in the missing synonym to complete the analogy.

| loyal   country   winner |
| site   restore |

1. change : alter :: renew : _____
2. village : town :: place : _____
3. city : metropolis :: nation : _____
4. careful : cautious :: faithful : _____
5. answer : solution :: victor : _____

Name/Date _____

## Vocabulary: Synonyms and Antonyms 4

Fill in the missing letters in the antonyms that complete each analogy.

1. happy : sad :: joyful : d _ _ r _ ss _ d
2. tragic : comic :: cry : l _ _ _ h
3. enemy : friend :: dislike : l _ k _
4. lose : gain :: give : t _ _ e
5. white : black :: colorful : color _ _ _ _

Name/Date _____

## Vocabulary: Synonyms and Antonyms 5

Use the clue to unscramble the last synonym in each analogy.

1. distant : far :: close : _____ earn
2. revise : correct :: mature : _____ rogw
3. right : correct :: error : _____ estamik
4. story : tale :: poem : _____ eersv
5. large : big :: small : _____ tillet

# Analogies Warm-ups:
# Vocabulary Analogies: Homophones

Name/Date _____

## Vocabulary: Homophones 1

Circle the missing word.

1. ate : eight :: won : zeroonesingle
2. dear : deer :: bare : revealshowbear
3. blew : blue :: read : orangeredyellow
4. meet : meat :: bred : slicebreadfrom
5. hole : whole :: peace : pieceslicedove

Name/Date _____

## Vocabulary: Homophones 2

Draw a line to match the word to the analogy.

1. mist : missed :: past :          site
2. made : maid :: hare :           nose
3. pause : paws : clause :         passed
4. cent : sent :: cite :           claws
5. clothes : close :: knows :      hair

Name/Date _____

## Vocabulary: Homophones 3

On your own paper, write each analogy in words. (Example: mail : male :: sail : sale is written as "mail is to male as sail is to sale")

1. oar : ore :: soar : sore
2. here : hear :: herd : heard
3. heal : heel :: real : reel
4. lead : led :: read : red
5. peek : peak :: week : weak

Name/Date _____

## Vocabulary: Homophones 4

Use the clue to unscramble the last word in each analogy.

1. pain : pane :: main : _____ mean
2. tail : tale :: sail : _____ laes
3. toad : towed :: road : _____ rwedo
4. who's : whose :: you'll : _____ luey
5. right : write :: read : _____ rdee

Name/Date _____

## Vocabulary: Homophones 5

Use the choices to fill in the correct word.

1. be : bee :: aunt : _____
2. beat : beet :: carat : _____
3. two : to :: four : _____
4. knew : new :: knot : _____
5. pole : poll :: role : _____

sister relative ant

carrot jewel weight

eight for quarter

tie know not

roll actor part

# Analogies Warm-ups: Vocabulary Analogies: Suffixes

---

Name/Date _____

## Vocabulary: Suffixes 1

Circle the word with the suffix that best completes the analogy.

1. comfort : comfortable :: perish :        perished        find        perishable

2. teach : teacher :: work :        worker        play        worked

3. write : writer :: read :        reading        red        reader

4. act : actor :: edit :        editor        acting        editing

5. sell : seller :: buy :        purchase        buyer        buying

---

Name/Date _____

## Vocabulary: Suffixes 2

On your own paper, write each analogy in words. (Example: slow : slower :: quick : quicker is written as "slow is to slower as quick is to quicker")

1. strength : strengthen :: length : lengthen

2. light : lighter :: dark : darker

3. lucky : luckier :: happy : happier

4. soft : softest :: hard : hardest

5. boy : boyish :: girl : girlish

---

Name/Date _____

## Vocabulary: Suffixes 3

Match each word to the correct analogy.

1. use : useless :: age : _____

2. brother : brotherly :: sister : _____

3. weary : weariness :: happy : _____

4. fearless : fearlessness :: artless : _____

5. kind : kindness :: dark : _____

a. darkness     b. artlessness     c. sisterly
d. ageless     e. happiness

---

Name/Date _____

## Vocabulary: Suffixes 4

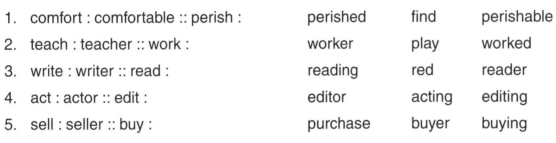

Fill in the missing letters.

1. friend : friendship :: citizen:
   _ _ _ _ _ _ _ ship

2. good : goodness :: sad : sad _ _ _ _

3. friend : friendly :: sad : _ _ _ ly

4. laugh : laughing :: cry : cry _ _ _

5. add : addition :: divide : divis _ _ _

---

Name/Date _____

## Vocabulary: Suffixes 5

Write the missing word to complete the analogy.

1. create : creative :: act : _____

2. enjoy : enjoyment :: excite : _____

3. hope : hopeless :: life : _____

4. truth : truthful :: fear : _____

5. slave : slavery :: brave : _____

---

# Analogies Warm-ups: Vocabulary Analogies: Prefixes

Name/Date _____

## Vocabulary: Prefixes 1

Underline the word with a prefix that completes the analogy.

1. invent : reinvent :: write : reportnlkrewrite
2. active : inactive :: complete : termincompletereact
3. believe : disbelieve :: appear : resdisappeardislike
4. fiction : nonfiction :: profit : plortbsnonprofitonfelk

Name/Date _____

## Vocabulary: Prefixes 2

Draw a line to match each word with the correct analogy.

1. view : preview :: heat :            misunderstand
2. national : international :: state :   preheat
3. done : overdone :: spend :          recopy
4. read : misread :: understand :      interstate
5. appear : reappear :: copy :         overspend

Name/Date _____

## Vocabulary: Prefixes 3

Fill in the missing letters.

1. select : preselect :: cut : pre _ _ _
2. arrange : rearrange :: pay : _ _ pay
3. lock : unlock :: solved : _ _ solved
4. last : outlast :: perform : _ _ _ perform

Name/Date _____

## Vocabulary: Prefixes 4

Write the missing word with a prefix that completes each analogy.

1. way : subway :: marine : _____
2. circle : semicircle :: finals : _____
3. healthy : unhealthy :: true : _____
4. cover : undercover :: ground : _____

Name/Date _____

_____

## Vocabulary: Prefixes 5

Unscramble the last word in each analogy.

1. polite : impolite :: patient : pimnatiet

_____

2. sensitive : insensitive :: perfect : ipecmerft

_____

3. responsible : irresponsible :: regular : ulrraiegr

_____

4. mature : immature :: possible : isiblsmpoe

_____

5. visible : invisible :: attention : iionnatentt

_____

# Analogies Warm-ups:
# Vocabulary Analogies: Greek and Latin Roots

---

Name/Date _____

## Vocabulary: Greek and Latin Roots 1

Circle the best choice.

1. photograph : light :: phonograph :
   camera      film      sound
2. bicycle : two :: tricycle :
   five        three      wheel
3. telephone : hearing :: television :
   sight      distant      monitor
4. telescope : far :: microscope :
   large      vision      small

---

Name/Date _____

## Vocabulary: Greek and Latin Roots 2

Draw a line to match the word to the analogy.

1. tripod : foot :: triangle :          eat
2. unicycle : wheel :: uniform :        shape
3. manicure : hand :: pedicure :        turn
4. insecticide : kill :: insectivore :  corner
5. construct : build :: revolve :       foot

---

Name/Date _____

## Vocabulary: Greek and Latin Roots 3

Fill in the blank to complete the analogy.

1. pedestrian : walker :: equestrian : _____

2. telegraph : write :: telephone : _____

3. quadruped : feet :: quadrangle : _____

4. friction : rubbed :: fraction : _____

5. dentist : tooth :: podiatrist : _____

**foot
corners
speak
broken
rider**

---

Name/Date _____

## Vocabulary: Greek and Latin Roots 4

Fill in the missing letters.

1. nativity : birth :: mortality : de _ _ _

2. solar : sun :: lunar : m _ _ n

3. eject : out :: inject : _ _

4. maternal : mother :: paternal : fa _ _ _ r

5. import : in :: export : _ _ _

---

Name/Date _____

## Vocabulary: Greek and Latin Roots 5

Unscramble the last word in each analogy.

1. export : carry :: extend : trchest

   _____

2. junction : join :: donation : geiv

   _____

3. altimeter : height :: barometer : rresepsu

   _____

4. minimum : less :: maximum : meor

   _____

# Analogies Warm-ups: Vocabulary Analogies: Clipped Words

Name/Date _____

## Vocabulary: Clipped Words 1

Circle the best full word that completes the analogy featuring clipped words.

1. ad : advertisement :: memo :
   mention  motion  memorandum
2. gas : gasoline :: flu :
   influenza  fluent  virus
3. tux : tuxedo :: vet :
   vegetable  veterinarian  doctor
4. burger : hamburger :: lab :
   place  laboratory  scientist

Name/Date _____

## Vocabulary: Clipped Words 2

Fill in the missing letters.

1. phone : telephone :: copter :
   _ _ li _ _ p _ _ r
2. photo : photograph :: teen : t _ _ n _ g _ r
3. gym : gymnasium :: fan : fa _ _ t _ _
4. cab : taxicab :: van : ca _ _ v _ _
5. exam : examination :: dorm :
   do _ _ it _ _ _

Name/Date _____

## Vocabulary: Clipped Words 3

Match each word to the correct analogy.

1. auto : automobile :: math : _____
2. auto : automobile :: bike : _____
3. lunch : luncheon :: fridge : _____
4. fax : facsimile :: lube : _____
5. asst. : assistant :: ft. : _____

a. lubricate  b. foot  c. bicycle
d. mathematics  e. refrigerator

Name/Date _____

## Vocabulary: Clipped Words 4

Write the correct word on the line.

1. copter : helicopter :: auto : _____
2. limo : limousine :: stereo : _____
3. pants : pantaloons :: tie : _____
4. champ : champion :: doc : _____
5. plane : airplane :: bus : _____

| doctor | omnibus | stereophonic |
| necktie | automobile | |

Name/Date _____

## Vocabulary: Clipped Words 5

Unscramble the word that completes the analogy. Write it on the line.

1. ref : referee :: grad : _____  agrteadu

2. rhino : rhinoceros :: hippo : _____  ipothusopapm

3. deli : delicatessen :: sub : _____  bsunemari

4. quake : earthquake :: prof : _____  roprsofes

5. piano : pianoforte :: cell : _____  lulacelr

# Analogies Warm-ups:
# Vocabulary Analogies: Acronyms

Name/Date _____

_____

## Vocabulary: Acronyms 1

Underline the missing word that completes each analogy. The word will be the word represented by the last letter in each acronym.

1. ZIP : plan :: RAM :

   rowpkmomemorystem

2. RIP : peace :: TBA :

   beginameannouncedstand

3. UFO : object :: UPS :

   puposservicereceiver

4. RADAR : range :: SCUBA :

   belowunderapparatustable

5. SASE : envelope :: SWAT :

   winterseasonteamlaterafter

Name/Date _____

## Vocabulary: Acronyms 2

Circle the best choice to complete the analogy.

1. ATM : machine :: ASAP :     after   never   possible
2. ESL : language :: EU :       union   ever   usual
3. CD : disc :: DJ :            juice   Denver   jockey
4. SUV : vehicle :: SOS :       sunny   ship   over
5. TLC : care :: DVR :          recorder   cover   very

Name/Date _____

## Vocabulary: Acronyms 3

Match to complete the anaolgy.

1. VIP : person :: POW : ____      a. view
2. PTA : association :: POV : ____  b. computer
3. PS : script :: RV : ____         c. operandi
4. PR : relations :: PC : ____      d. war
5. RSVP : plait :: MO : ____        e. vehicle

Name/Date _____

## Vocabulary: Acronyms 4

Fill in the missing letters.

1. NASA : administration :: PIN : n _ m _ _ r
2. LOL : loud :: MRI : i _ _ g _ _ g
3. HQ : quarters :: IQ : q _ _ t _ _ _ t
4. FBI : investigation : IRS : s _ _ v _ c _
5. HIV : virus :: FYI : i _ _ o _ _ a _ _ _ n

Name/Date _____

## Vocabulary: Acronyms 5

Unscramble. The word may be any word in the acronym.

1. BLT : tomato :: CEO : _____ oerffic
2. ERA : rights :: CIA : _____ ielnenctlige
3. PA : public :: HQ : _____ adhe
4. CEO : executive :: DVD : _____ idvoe
5. COD : cash :: GPA : _____ readg

# Analogies Warm-ups:
# Vocabulary Analogies: Portmanteau Words

Name/Date _____

## Vocabulary: Portmanteau Words 1

Circle the best choice to complete each analogy.

1. bash : smash :: botch :        beach   blotch   ruin
2. blow : blurt :: splash :        wash   splutter   puddle
3. cinema : cinemaplex :: emotion :    Internet   message   emoticon
4. flop : drop :: brunch :        lunch   crunch   dinner
5. Frankenfood : Frankenstein ::

   docudrama :            film   book   documentary

> Portmanteau words are new words made up of a combination of two or more other words. In each analogy, you will either be looking for one of the original words, or you will be given a word and asked to find the portmanteau word.

---

Name/Date _____

## Vocabulary: Portmanteau Words 2

| a. software   b. spatter |
| c. communication   d. stumble   e. rash |

Match to complete the analogy.

1. blog : log :: brash : _____
2. beefalo : buffalo :: bumble : _____
3. camcorder : recorder :: freeware : _____
4. glitz : ritz :: splatter : _____
5. hazmat : materials :: intercom : _____

---

Name/Date _____

## Vocabulary: Portmanteau Words 3

| a. snort     b. short     c. complex |
| d. element   e. care |

Match to complete the analogy.

1. Internet : network :: Medicare : _____
2. motel : hotel :: multiplex : _____
3. pang : sting :: pixel : _____
4. scrunch : crunch :: skort : _____
5. smog : fog :: chortle : _____

---

Name/Date _____

## Vocabulary: Portmanteau Words 4

Fill in the missing letters.

1. guesstimate : estimate :: infomercial :
   c _ _ m _ r _ _ _ _
2. telethon : marathon :: sitcom :
   _ o _ _ _ y
3. Skylab : laboratory :: slang :
   l _ _ gu _ _e
4. slosh : slush :: smash : m _ _ _
5. grumble : rumble :: glop : s _ _ p

---

Name/Date _____

## Vocabulary: Portmanteau Words 5

On your own paper, write each analogy in words. (Example: blog : log :: Internet : network is written as "blog is to log as Internet is to network")

1. squiggle : wiggle :: telethon : marathon
2. pulsar : star :: bionic : electronic
3. stagflation : inflation :: netiquette : ettiquette
4. swipe : sweep :: splatter : splash

---

# Analogies Warm-ups:
# Grammar Analogies: Irregular Verb Forms

Name/Date _____

## Grammar: Irregular Verb Forms 1

Circle the best choice.

1. am : are :: was :         have  is  were
2. build : built :: catch :     release  caught  trap
3. feed : fed :: freeze :     froze  thaw  cold
4. fight : fought :: bring :    brought  brang  bringed
5. do : did :: get :         gave  obtain  got

Name/Date _____

## Grammar: Irregular Verb Forms 2

Fill in the missing letters to complete the anaolgy.

1. eat : ate :: has : h _ _
2. draw : drew :: fly : _ _ _ w
3. forgive : forgave :: drink : dr _ _ _
4. hit : hit :: cut : _ _ t
5. light : lit :: bite : _ _ _

Name/Date _____

## Grammar: Irregular Verb Forms 3

Draw lines to match the words to the correct analogy.

1. do : did :: eat :         felt
2. bend : bent :: bleed :    bled
3. choose : chose :: drink :   broke
4. dig : dug :: feel :       drank
5. forget : forgot :: break :   ate

Name/Date _____

## Grammar: Irregular Verb Forms 4

Unscramble the word to complete each analogy.

1. lay : laid :: lie : _____ yal
2. run : ran :: say : _____ isda
3. see : saw :: sell : _____ dlso
4. shoot : shot :: shake : _____ osokh

Name/Date _____

_____

## Grammar: Irregular Verb Forms 5

Circle the missing word.

1. know : knew :: grow :

   groweddgrewgrowt

2. hear : heard :: make :

   makedmademaidmaker

3. ride : rode :: rise :

   risedroserededrice

4. shake : shook :: take :

   takedtooktakerteektike

5. has : had :: mean :

   meantmeanedmeand

# Analogies Warm-ups:
# Grammar Analogies: Parts of Speech

---

Name/Date _____

## Grammar: Parts of Speech 1

Circle the missing word.

1. table : noun :: go :    adjective verb noun
2. yellow : adjective :: slowly : pronoun verb adverb
3. walk : verb :: path :   noun adjective verb
4. loudly : adverb :: loud : adverb adjective noun
5. good : adjective :: well : verb adjective adverb

---

Name/Date _____

## Grammar: Parts of Speech 2

Fill in the word that completes each analogy.

1. loud : loudly :: good : _____
2. quick : quickly :: slow : _____
3. happy : happily :: merry : _____
4. hungry : hungrily :: greedy : _____

| | | | |
|---|---|---|---|
| **greedily** | **well** | **slowly** | **merrily** |

---

Name/Date _____

## Grammar: Parts of Speech 3

Match to complete the analogy.

1. careful : carefully :: hopeful : ____
2. easy : easily :: weary : ____
3. bright : brightly :: bad : ____
4. usual : usually :: helpful : ____
5. deep : deeply :: kind : ____

    a. kindly       b. helpfully     c. wearily
    d. hopefully    e. badly

---

Name/Date _____

## Grammar: Parts of Speech 4

Fill in the missing letters.

1. gentle : adjective :: gently : a _ _ _ _ b
2. love : noun :: lovable : _ d _ _ c _ i _ _
3. peacefully : adverb :: peace : n _ _ _
4. rider : noun :: riding : _ _ r _
5. tight : adjective :: tighter :
   a _ _ e _ _ _ v _

---

Name/Date _____

## Grammar: Parts of Speech 5

Unscramble the word to complete the analogy.

1. noisy : noisily :: lazy : _____        zilayl
2. rare : rarely :: nice : _____        nelyic
3. jealous : jealously :: needless : _____        ednelelyss
4. legal : legally :: internal : _____        lntinaerly
5. bashful : bashfully :: delightful : _____        dehltfulligy

---

# Analogies Warm-ups:
# Phonics Analogies: Long and Short Vowels

Name/Date _____

## Phonics: Long and Short Vowels 1

Circle the best choice to complete each analogy.

1. hate : hat :: cane :        candy        can        walking
2. car : care :: far :         fare         near       distant
3. cap : cape :: tap :         hit          touch      tape
4. glad : glade :: mad :       made         angry      maddening
5. grad : grade :: fad :       dance        fade       fashion

---

Name/Date _____

## Phonics: Long and Short Vowels 2

Fill in the word to complete each analogy.

1. man : mane :: pan : _____
2. van : vane :: plan : _____
3. mat : mate :: rat : _____
4. past : paste :: star : _____
5. kit : kite :: bit : _____

Name/Date _____

## Phonics: Long and Short Vowels 3

Draw a line to match the word with the analogy.

1. hid : hide :: rid :          spine
2. grim : grime :: slim :       slime
3. dim : dime :: prim :         pine
4. fin : fine :: spin :         prime
5. shin : shine :: pin :        ride

---

Name/Date _____

## Phonics: Long and Short Vowels 4

Unscramble the missing word in the analogy.

1. twin : twine :: grip : _____ ipgre
2. quit : quite :: sit : _____ itse
3. rob : robe :: glob : _____ gelob
4. hop : hope :: slop : _____ peslo
5. not : note :: tot :: _____ teot

Name/Date _____

## Phonics: Long and Short Vowels 5

On your own paper, write the following analogies in words. (Example: bit : bite :: mit : mite is written as "bit is to bite as mit is to mite")

1. hug : huge :: cut : cute
2. slat : slate :: scrap : scrape
3. gap : gape :: tap : tape
4. ton : tone :: mop : mope
5. spit : spite :: fir : fire

# Analogies Warm-ups:
# Phonics Analogies: Blends and Digraphs

## Phonics: Blends and Digraphs 1

Circle the missing word to complete the analogy.

1. blue : true :: blend :    black    mix    trend
2. cheat : treat :: chip :    piece    trip    chocolate
3. tree : flee :: try :    fly    succeed    true
4. snow : glow :: snob :    snow    glob    superior
5. stop : shop :: store :    shore    shop    stop

## Phonics: Blends and Digraphs 2

Fill in the missing word to complete the analogy.

1. now : snow :: nap : _____
2. his : this :: hen : _____
3. rim : trim :: rail : _____
4. hip : ship :: hop : _____
5. car : scar :: core : _____

## Phonics: Blends and Digraphs 3

Draw a line to match the word to the correct analogy.

1. low : slow :: lid :    gray
2. mall : small :: mash :    plot
3. lace : place :: lot :    knob
4. new : knew :: nob :    smash
5. rain : grain :: ray :    slid

## Phonics: Blends and Digraphs 4

Fill in the missing letters.

1. grad : grand :: lad : l _ _ d
2. cat : cast :: mat : m _ _ t
3. wit : with :: bat : b _ _ _
4. rig : ring :: wig : w _ _ _
5. pat : past :: wet : w _ _ _

## Phonics: Blends and Digraphs 5

Circle the missing letters. The letters will be the blend or digraph found in the second word in the analogy.

1. telescope : sc :: asleep :

   trsxbbsletyoon

2. muskrat : sk :: sunshine :

   istyryattresshoe

3. April : pr :: respect :

   ispoltruckngshmr

4. destroy : st :: patrol :

   ngrtesplntrenmon

5. father : th :: singer :

   pltrockngldltrd

# Analogies Warm-ups:
# Literature Analogies: Poetic Devices

---

Name/Date _____

## Literature: Poetic Devices 1

On your own paper, write the following analogies in words. (Example: cricket : chirp :: chick : cheep is written as "cricket is to chirp as chick is to cheep")

1. horse : neigh :: dog : bow-wow
2. pig : oink :: duck : quack
3. frog : ribbit :: cat : meow
4. cow : moo :: sheep : baa
5. donkey : heehaw :: chicken : cluck

---

Name/Date _____

## Literature: Poetic Devices 2

Match the word to the correct analogy.

1. snore : zzzzzzzz :: sneeze : ____
2. clock : tick :: door : ____
3. bored : ho-hum :: laugh : ____
4. water : gurgle :: fire : ____
5. explode : boom :: guitar : ____

a. knock    b. crackle    c. twang
d. haha     e. achoo

---

Name/Date _____

## Literature: Poetic Devices 3

Circle the best choice to complete each analogy.

1. disappointed : boo :: cold :        hot        chilly        brrrrh

2. doorbell : buzz :: bell :           bronze     ding          tower

3. scared : eek :: train :             chug       railroad      plane

4. cheer : hurrah :: quiet :           song       shhh          sound

5. tasty : yum :: distasteful :        tasty      unpleasant    yuck

---

Name/Date _____

## Literature: Poetic Devices 4

Fill in the missing letters.

1. late : rate :: low : r _ _
2. fought : bought :: fudge : b _ d _ e
3. mush : rush :: mow : r _ _
4. house : mouse :: hound : m _ _ _ d
5. dust : trust :: duck : tr _ _ _

---

Name/Date _____

## Literature: Poetic Devices 5

Use the clue to unscramble the second word in each pair.

1. dear : hear :: net: _____ tpe
2. funny : money :: had : _____ dda
3. clean : mean :: bag : _____ arg
4. alliteration : beginning :: rhyme : _____ den
5. paragraph : prose :: stanza : _____ moep

---

# Analogies Warm-ups:
# Literature Analogies: Narrative Elements

Name/Date _____

## Literature: Narrative Elements 1

Circle the best choice to complete each analogy.

| | | | |
|---|---|---|---|
| 1. Charlotte : character :: farm : | plot | setting | climax |
| 2. desert : setting :: argument : | conflict | character | protagonist |
| 3. school : setting :: Harry : | setting | time | character |
| 4. loneliness : problem :: friendship : | resolution | character | setting |
| 5. found : resolution :: lost : | character | plot | problem |

---

Name/Date _____

## Literature: Narrative Elements 2

Fill in the word to complete each analogy.

1. Charlotte : farm :: character : _____
2. poverty : wealth :: problem : _____
3. setting : past :: problem : _____
4. Harry : character :: unappreciated :

_____

| | |
|---|---|
| **poverty** | **resolution** |
| **problem** | **setting** |

---

Name/Date _____

## Literature: Narrative Elements 3

Match the word to the correct analogy.

1. school : setting :: Ramona : ____
2. humor : genre :: gratitude : ____
3. mystery : genre :: London : ____
4. fantasy : genre :: battle : ____
5. Huck : character :: rescue : ____

a. setting     b. resolution   c. conflict
d. character   e. theme

---

Name/Date _____

## Literature: Narrative Elements 4

Fill in the missing letters.
1. separated : problem :: reunited :
   r _ s _ l _ tion
2. Dorothy : character :: fantasy : g _ _ re
3. love : theme :: fight : c _ _ _ li _ t
4. separation : problem :: Land of Oz :
   se _ _ i _ g
5. country : setting :: Scarecrow :
   c _ _ r _ _ t _ r

---

Name/Date _____

## Literature: Narrative Elements 5

Unscramble the letters to complete the analogy.
1. Alice : character :: Wonderland : _____
   tinsetg
2. loss : problem :: recovery : _____
   etiorsolun
3. midnight : setting :: greed : _____ tehem
4. survival : problem :: historical : _____
   enrge

---

# Analogies Warm-ups: Literature Analogies: Parts of a Book

Name/Date _____

_____

## Literature: Parts of a Book 1

Circle the best choice to complete each analogy.

1. name : person :: title :

   place    number    book

2. chapter : book :: sentence :

   word    paragraph    letter

3. definition : glossary ::

   page number :

   fifteen    place    index

4. alphabetical : index ::

   sequence :

   order    contents    next

5. index : end :: introduction :

   conclusion    introduce

   beginning

Name/Date _____

## Literature: Parts of a Book 2

Fill in with the best choice to complete each analogy.

1. preface : before :: appendix : _____
2. book : chapter :: heading : _____
3. clothes : person :: cover : _____
4. information : chapter :: definition : _____

| book | glossary | after | subheading |

Name/Date _____

## Literature: Parts of a Book 3

Draw a line to match the word with the correct analogy.

1. word : dictionary :: map :          almanac
2. sentence : paragraph :: chapter :   caption
3. film : narration :: picture :       book
4. town : overlook :: subject :        encyclopedia
5. map : atlas :: statistics :         atlas

Name/Date _____

## Literature: Parts of a Book 4

Fill in the missing letters to complete the analogy.

1. poetry : prose :: fiction : _ _ _ fict _ _ n
2. anthology : collection :: novel : f _ c _ _ _ n
3. sign : street :: guideword : d _ _ t _ _ n _ _ y
4. biography : nonfiction :: map : di _ _ r _ m
5. drawing : model :: map : gl _ _ e

Name/Date _____

## Literature: Parts of a Book 5

Unscramble the word to complete the analogy.

1. book : catalog :: topic : _____ iexnd
2. encyclopedia : guide word :: Internet : _____ rkodeyw
3. history : nonfiction :: fantasy : _____ ctifino
4. glossary : vocabulary :: bibliography : _____ esursoc

# Analogies Warm-ups: Science Analogies: Sequence

---

Name/Date _____

## Science: Sequence 1

Circle the best choice.

1. clay : shale :: sand :          particle       beach       sandstone
2. limestone : marble :: shale :  slate          hard        sedimentary
3. magma : basalt :: ash :        volcanic       porous      tuff
4. sand : sandstone :: shell :    organic        marine      fossil

---

Name/Date _____

## Science: Sequence 2

On your own paper, write the following analogies in words. (Example: fruit : seed :: seed : sprout is written as "fruit is to seed as seed is to sprout")

1. seed : sprout :: sprout : stem   2. pollen : seed :: seed : sprout   3. leaf : bud :: bud : flower

4. light : photosynthesis :: photosynthesis : food       5. bud : flower :: flower : fruit

---

Name/Date _____

## Science: Sequence 3

Complete each analogy with the best word.

1. rain : puddle :: puddle : _____   2. rising : vapor :: cooling : _____

3. warm : rises :: cool : _____   4. cloud : charge :: lightning : _____

5. precipitation : evaporation :: evaporation : _____

a. condensation
b. replaces
c. thunder
d. dry
e. cloud

---

Name/Date _____

## Science: Sequence 4

Fill in the missing letters to complete the analogy.

1. sunrise : noon :: noon : s _ _ _ _ t        2. full: quarter :: crescent : n _ _

3. new : crescent :: quarter : _ _ _ _        4. dusk : midnight :: midnight : d _ _ n

5. summer : autumn :: winter : s _ _ _ _ g

---

Name/Date _____

## Science: Sequence 5

Use the clue to fill in the missing letters in the last word in each analogy.

1. rubbing : friction :: friction : h _ _ _        2. sunlight : plant :: plant : h _ _ b _ _ ore

3. seeds : mouse :: mouse : h _ _ k        4. caterpillar : cocoon :: cocoon : m _ _ _

5. plant : herbivore :: herbivore : c _ _ n _ _ o _ e

---

# Analogies Warm-ups:
# Science Analogies: Part/Whole

Name/Date _____

## Science: Part/Whole 1

Fill in the best choice to complete each analogy.

1. baleen : whale :: fangs : _____
2. mane : lion :: antlers : _____
3. claws : cat :: talons : _____
4. horn : rhino :: shell : _____
5. camel : hump :: elephant : _____

> **deer   trunk   tortoise   snake   eagle**

Name/Date _____

## Science: Part/Whole 2

Draw a line to match the word to the analogy.

1. cone : pine :: acorn :          cell
2. leaf : maple :: needle :        lobster
3. bill : duck :: teeth :          fir
4. teeth : beaver :: claws :       alligator
5. proton : atom :: DNA :          oak

Name/Date _____

## Science: Part/Whole 3

Fill in the missing letters.

1. arms : starfish :: stinger : r _ _
2. flipper : seal :: antler : d _ _ r
3. fin : shark :: tusk : w _ _ r _ _
4. stripes : tiger :: spots : l _ _ p _ r _
5. fur : rabbit :: scales : sn _ _ _

Name/Date _____

## Science: Part/Whole 4

Unscramble the last word to complete the analogy.

1. fulcrum : lever :: wind : _____
   rericahun
2. crest : wave :: rope : _____ peully
3. moraine : glacier :: trunk : _____ tere
4. leaf : herb :: root : _____ lantp
5. shell : snail :: feather : _____ idrb

Name/Date _____

## Science: Part/Whole 5

Circle the best choice to complete each analogy.

1. leg : animal :: leaf :           green      lettuce    plant
2. caldera : volcano :: equator :   planet     equal      poles
3. pole : magnet :: face :          crystal    flat       edge
4. plate : crust :: tree :          pine       forest     trunk
5. antenna : ant :: whiskers :      walrus     smooth     prickly

# Analogies Warm-ups:
# Science Analogies: Greek and Latin Roots

Name/Date _____

## Science: Greek and Latin Roots 1

Circle the best choice to complete each analogy.

| | | | | |
|---|---|---|---|---|
| 1. | seismology : earthquakes :: geology : | life | stars | earth |
| 2. | mammology : mammals :: zoology : | plants | animals | parks |
| 3. | horticulture : cultivation :: botany : | plants | clothes | animals |
| 4. | cosmology : universe :: astronomy : | earth | fortunes | stars |
| 5. | climatology : climate :: meteorology : | meteorites | ecology | weather |

---

Name/Date _____

## Science: Greek and Latin Roots 2

On your own paper, write the word from the box that completes each analogy.
1. distance : telescope :: color :
2. microphone : sound :: microscope :
3. photograph : mark :: photosynthesis :
4. cardiology : heart :: psychology :
5. biome : ecosystem :: abiotic :

| make | mind | nonliving |
|---|---|---|
| spectroscope | sight | |

---

Name/Date _____

## Science: Greek and Latin Roots 3

Draw a line to match the word to the analogy.
1. star : interstellar :: galaxy :      lunar
2. solar : sun :: moon :                sail
3. stellar : star :: solar :            sky
4. terrestrial : land :: celestial :    sun
5. conduct : lead :: navigate :         intergalactic

---

Name/Date _____

## Science: Greek and Latin Roots 4

Fill in the missing letters.
1. geosphere : earth :: atmosphere : a _ _
2. hydrosphere : water :: geosphere :

    e _ _ _ h
3. atmosphere : air :: biosphere : l _ _ _
4. seismology : earthquake ::

    oceanography : o _ _ _ n

---

Name/Date _____

## Science: Greek and Latin Roots 5

On your own paper, write the following analogies in words. (Example: biology : life :: geology : earth is written as "biology is to life as geology is to earth")
1. chronometer : time :: thermometer : heat
2. photograph : mark :: photosynthesis : make
3. cycle : circle :: phobia : fear
4. geology : earth :: hydrology : water
5. optical : eye :: audible : ear

# Analogies Warm-ups:
# Science Analogies: Object/Class

---

Name/Date _____

## Science: Object/Class 1

Circle the best choice.

1. sandstone : sedimentary :: marble :
   hard   metamorphic   igneous
2. Jupiter : planet :: rose :
   flower   white   petals
3. oxygen : element :: water :
   compound   river   rain
4. oak : tree :: clam :
   shell   marine   bivalve

---

Name/Date _____

## Science: Object/Class 2

Match the word to the analogy.

1. shark : fish :: seal : ____
2. eagle : bird :: tortoise : ____
3. bacteria : living :: basalt : ____
4. fern : plant :: beetle : ____
5. mushroom : fungus :: redwood : ____

   a. animal      b. tree    c. reptile
   d. nonliving   e. mammal

---

Name/Date _____

## Science: Object/Class 3

Fill in the correct word from the box to complete the analogy.

1. humpback : whale :: tiger : _____

2. lion : feline :: wolf : _____

3. mouse : herbivore :: hawk : _____

4. snake : reptile :: frog : _____

5. camel : domesticated :: hippopotamus : _____

| canine    amphibian |
| wild   carnivore   feline |

---

Name/Date _____

## Science: Object/Class 4

Use the clue to fill in the missing letters.

1. monkey : mammal :: shark : _ _ s _
2. frog : amphibian :: lizard : r _ _ _ _ _ e
3. water : nonliving :: germ : l _ _ i _ g
4. spider : animal :: daisy : _ _ a _ t
5. pine : tree :: toadstool : f _ _ _ _ s

---

Name/Date _____

## Science: Object/Class 5

Use the clue to unscramble the last word in each analogy, and write the answer on your own paper.

1. lever : machine :: hurricane : sormt
2. sun : star :: pulley : chaeinm
3. steam : gas :: ice : liods
4. snake : vertebrate :: worm : vbraterteine
5. snail : exoskeleton :: dog : eseleonktndo

---

# Analogies Warm-ups: Geography Analogies: Part/Whole

Name/Date _____

## Geography: Part/Whole 1

Circle the best choice to complete the analogy.

1. bank : stream :: shore :        coast        lake
2. neighborhood : city :: city :        state        Denver
3. city : state :: state :        county        country
4. country : continent :: continent : hemisphere        island
5. summit : mountain :: bed :        bottom        river

Name/Date _____

## Geography: Part/Whole 2

Match each relationship to the correct analogy.

1. ridge : ocean :: mountains : _____        a. neighborhood
2. river : valley :: current : _____        b. ocean
3. path : garden :: trail : _____        c. state
4. house : block :: block : _____        d. wilderness
5. province : nation :: town : _____        e. land

Name/Date _____

## Geography: Part/Whole 3

Use the clue to fill in the missing letters.

1. tree : forest :: dunes : d _ _ _ _ t
2. ice : glacier :: water : r _ _ _ r
3. stalactite : cave :: crater : v _ _ _ _ _ o
4. forest : biosphere :: lake : hy _ _ _ s _ _ _ re

Name/Date _____

## Geography: Part/Whole 4

Unscramble the word to complete the analogy.

1. seasons : climate :: precipitation : _____ aterhwe
2. population : census :: area : _____ rvseuy
3. grass : plains :: cactus : _____ edtser
4. valley : hills :: canyon : _____ lautepa

Name/Date _____

_____

## Geography: Part/Whole 5

Circle the missing word.

1. neighborhood : city :: block :

    house    square    neighborhood

2. road : country :: street :

    ohr    town    main    paved    turn

3. state : region :: region :

    west    country    large    wontrs

4. trench : ocean :: gorge :

    peak    deep    mountains    flat

5. farm : country :: factory :

    manufacturing    auto    city

# Analogies Warm-ups:
# Geography Analogies: Object/Class

---

Name/Date _____

## Geography: Object/Class 1

On your own paper, write the following analogies in words. (Example: Denali : mountain :: Rio Grande : river is written as "Denali is to mountain as Rio Grande is to river")

1. Maui : island :: Everest : mountain
2. Pacific : ocean :: Baja : peninsula
3. Africa : continent :: Hawaii : island
4. Mojave : desert :: Atlantic : ocean
5. Erie : lake :: Columbia : river

---

Name/Date _____

## Geography: Object/Class 2

Fill in the correct word from the box.

1. Nile : river :: Arctic : _____
2. Antarctica : continent :: Amazon : _____
3. Mississippi : river :: Sahara : _____
4. California : state :: Canada : _____
5. Mediterranean : sea :: Monterey : _____

| desert   bay   nation   river   ocean |

---

Name/Date _____

## Geography: Object/Class 3

Match to complete the analogy.

1. Hudson : bay :: Colorado : ____
2. Chicago : city :: Spain : ____
3. Australia : continent :: Maui : ____
4. Atlantic : ocean :: Danube : ____
5. Caribbean : sea :: Appalachians : ____

   a. river      b. nation    c. mountains
   d. island     e. state

---

Name/Date _____

## Geography: Object/Class 4

Fill in the missing letters.

1. Antigua : island :: Red : _ _ a
2. Black : forest :: Tigris : r _ _ _ r
3. London : city :: UK : na _ _ _ _
4. Germany : nation :: Europe :
   c _ _ t _ n _ n _
5. Spain : nation :: Madrid : c _ _ _

---

Name/Date _____

## Geography: Object/Class 5

Unscramble the word to complete each analogy.

1. Asia : continent :: India : _____ nnioat
2. France : nation :: French : _____ ngugeala
3. Rhine : river :: Alps : _____ untinsamo
4. equator : latitude :: Prime Meridian : _____ gndeitulo
5. Nebraska : state :: Platte : _____ verri

---

# Analogies Warm-ups:
# Geography Analogies: Object/Place

---

Name/Date _____

## Geography: Object/Place 1

Circle the best choice.

1. Golden Gate : San Francisco ::
   Grand Canyon :   park   river   Arizona
2. Big Ben : London :: Eiffel Tower :
   Paris   famous   France
3. Arches : Utah :: Yosemite :
   waterfall   scenic   California
4. Hoover Dam : Nevada :: Vesuvius :
   Italy   Naples   volcano

---

Name/Date _____

## Geography: Object/Place 2

Match the best word to each analogy.

1. kangaroo : Australia :: bison : ____
2. Harvard : USA :: Oxford : ____
3. tiger : India :: lion : ____
4. Altamira Cave : Spain ::
   Carlsbad Caverns : ____
5. camel : North Africa :: albatross : ____

a. Africa  b. USA  c. England
d. Galapagos Islands  e. USA

---

Name/Date _____

## Geography: Object/Place 3

Fill in the word from the box that completes the analogy.

1. buzzards : Hinckley :: swallows : _____

2. Parthenon : Athens :: Forum : _____

3. White House : Washington, D.C. :: Empire State Building :

   _____

4. iceberg : arctic :: Kilauea : _____

5. Stonehenge : England :: pyramids : _____

| New York |
| Eygpt |
| Hawaii |
| Capistrano |
| Rome |

---

Name/Date _____

## Geography: Object/Place 4

Fill in the missing letters.

1. tractor : farm :: elevator : c _ _ y
2. ship : ocean :: railroad : l _ _ d
3. street : city :: highway : st _ _ e
4. tortoise : desert :: turtle : p _ _ _
5. cactus : desert :: fir : m _ _ _ t _ _ n _

---

Name/Date _____

## Geography: Object/Place 5

Unscramble the last word to complete each analogy. Write the answers on your own paper.

1. spruce : forest :: kelp : oance
2. chicken : farm :: eagle : mtunnaios
3. fountain : city :: well : ntrcoyu
4. bear : mountains :: trout : trsema
5. penguin : Antarctica :: ostrich : riAafc

---

# Analogies Warm-ups:
# Geography Analogies: Object/Description

Name/Date _____

_____

## Geography: Object/ Description 1

Use the clue to unscramble the last word in the analogy.

1. weather : day ::

   climate : caeedd

   _____

2. street : short ::

   highway : onlg

   _____

3. butte : uplifted ::

   canyon : vdcear

   _____

4. delta : deposited ::

   valley : deerod

   _____

5. urban : industrial ::

   rural : ricuraaltugl

   _____

Name/Date _____

## Geography: Object/Description 2

On your own paper, write the following analogies in words. (Example: ocean : large :: lake : small is written as "ocean is to large as lake is to small")

1. Arctic : cold :: Sahara : hot
2. metropolis : large :: village : small
3. rain forest : wet :: desert : dry
4. plains : flat :: mountains : steep

Name/Date _____

## Geography: Object/Description 3

Fill in the best word to complete each analogy.

1. island : small :: continent : _____
2. ocean : large :: sea : _____
3. mountains : jagged :: hills : _____
4. cactus : spiny :: moss : _____

| velvety |
| small |
| rolling |
| large |

Name/Date _____

## Geography: Object/Description 4

Draw a line to match each word with the correct analogy.

1. cars : personal :: trains :          steep
2. mesa : flat-top :: mountain :        public
3. stream : narrow :: river :           wide
4. slope : gentle :: cliff :            high
5. trench : deep :: mountain :          peak

Name/Date _____

## Geography: Object/Description 5

Fill in the missing letters.

1. mountain : cool :: rain forest : _ _ _ m
2. grasslands : fertile :: badlands : b _ _ _ _ n
3. plateau : high :: basin : l _ _
4. lake : collecting :: stream : dr _ _ n _ _ g

# Analogies Warm-ups:
# Health Analogies: Part/Whole & Object/Class

Name/Date _____

## Health: Part/Whole 1

Circle the missing word to complete the analogy.

1. iris : eye :: finger :        armgonefoothandtoeelbowkneww

2. toe : foot :: knee :          legheadneckoranapplbana

3. skull : head :: vertebra :    toeearneckearmouthstngbackbone

4. tongue : mouth :: nostril :   pupiliristongyenosepalettetoothcanine

5. drum : ear :: jaw :           eartoeelbowkjneeskullnoseeyehairarnm

---

Name/Date _____

## Health: Part/Whole 2

Fill in the blanks with the missing word.

1. knee : leg :: elbow : _____
2. wrist : hand :: ankle : _____
3. neck : head :: waist : _____
4. shoulder : arm :: hip : _____
5. pupil : eye :: crown : _____

| leg   torso   foot   tooth   arm |
|---|

Name/Date _____

## Health: Part/Whole 3

Draw a line to match the word with the analogy.

1. chamber : heart :: lobe :       chest

2. roof : mouth :: canal :         skeleton

3. cochlea : ear :: ribs :         arms

4. lid : eye :: ribs :             ear

5. knuckles : fingers :: elbows :  lung

---

Name/Date _____

## Health: Object/Class 4

Fill in the missing letters.

1. walking : fitness ::
   vegetables : nu _ _ it _ _ n
2. potato : carbohydrate :: fish :
   p _ _ t _ _ n
3. cheese : dairy :: cereal : gr _ _ _ s
4. oats : grains :: milk : d _ _ _ y
5. peach : fruit :: carrot : v _ _ _ t _ _ le

Name/Date _____

## Health: Object/Class 5

Unscramble the last word in each analogy.

1. honey : sugar :: butter : _____ aft
2. dairy : nutrition :: swimming : _____
   tsnefis
3. milk : calcium :: cereal : _____ rbfie
4. broccoli : vegetable :: apple : _____ utifr
5. wheat : grains :: buttermilk : _____
   ayird

# Analogies Warm-ups:
# Health Analogies: Object/Function & Object/Description

Name/Date _____

## Health: Object/Function 1

Circle the best choice.

1. nerve : communicate :: stomach :
   digest     mouth     tongue
2. teeth : chew :: saliva :
   liquid     mouth     dissolve
3. skin : protect :: blood :
   red     deliver     type
4. skeleton : support :: knees :
   bend     legs     know

Name/Date _____

## Health: Object/Description 2

Match the best word to each analogy.

1. resistance : strength :: stretching : ____
2. repetition : endurance :: resistance : ____
3. drink : water :: breath : ____
4. talk : communication :: laugh : ____
5. food : energy :: sleep : ____

   a. oxygen  b. restoration  c. strength
   d. expression  e. flexibility

Name/Date _____

## Health: Object/Function 3

Fill in the word from the box that completes each analogy.

1. hands : hold :: feet : _____

2. muscles : move :: heart : _____

3. tendons : attach :: bladder : _____

4. lungs : breathe :: brain : _____

5. kidneys : filter :: arteries : _____

| pipe |
| pump |
| control |
| stand |
| collect |

Name/Date _____

## Health: Object/Function 4

Use the clue to fill in the missing letters.

1. tears : moisten :: perspiration : _ _ _ l
2. tongue : taste :: ear : b _ l _ _ c _
3. nutrition : health :: exercise :
   _ i _ _ s _
4. bed : sleep :: table : e _ _
5. park : play :: library : r _ _ _

Name/Date _____

## Health: Object/Description 5

Unscramble the word to complete the analogy.

1. vegetables : healthy :: donuts : atfinteng
   _____

2. biking : fast :: hiking : wlso _____
3. ball : rubber :: bat : odowne _____
4. television : passive :: skating : taciev
   _____

5. bandage : protect :: soap : dieficsnt
   _____

# Analogies Warm-ups:
# Health Analogies: Various Skills

Name/Date _____

## Health: Various Skills 1

Fill in with a word from the box to complete the analogy.
1. internal : external :: inside : _____
2. healthy : sick :: strong : _____
3. play : watch :: participant : _____
4. happy : sad :: energetic : _____

| weak | spectator | tired | outside |

Name/Date _____

## Health: Various Skills 2

Draw a line to match the word to the analogy.
1. microscopic : tiny :: large :         eye
2. resonance : echo :: graph :         thoughts
3. physical : body :: psychological :         mind
4. emotions : feelings :: ideas :         big
5. knows : nose :: I :         chart

Name/Date _____

## Health: Various Skills 3

Fill in the missing letters.
1. sea : see :: herd : h _ _ _ d
2. flew : flu :: horse : h _ _ _ _ e
3. nutrition : food :: exercise : a _ _ _ _ _ _ y
4. heel : heal :: feet : _ _ _ t
5. bad : bird :: foul : _ _ _ l

Name/Date _____

## Health: Various Skills 4

Unscramble the last word in each analogy.
1. here : hear :: site : tigsh _____
2. safe : dangerous :: harmless : rdhazusao _____
3. nontoxic : harmless :: toxic : mulfhar _____
4. tow : toe :: soar : osre _____

**DANGER!**

Name/Date _____

Name/Date _____

## Health: Various Skills 5

Circle the best choice.
1. chew : crush :: hinge :
    door
    steel
    bend
2. skeleton : framework ::
    network :
    system
    work
    restrain
3. visible : seen :: audible :
    auditorium
    touchable
    heard
4. elimination : removal ::
    respiration :
    breathing
    digestion
    movement
5. circulation : flow :: joint :
    skull
    knee
    meeting

# Analogies Warm-ups:
# Art and Music Analogies: Part/Whole & Object/Class

Name/Date _____

## Art and Music: Part/Whole 1

Circle the best choice.
1. peg : cello :: pedal :
   horn      volume      piano
2. stick : drum :: bow :
   violin      strings      rosin
3. violinist : orchestra :: trumpeter :
   player      metallic      band
4. president : company :: conductor :
   school      orchestra      hospital

Name/Date _____

## Art and Music: Object/Class 2

Fill in the analogy with a word from the box.
1. stroke : painting :: note : _____
2. landscape : painting :: concerto :
   _____
3. cello : strings :: trumpet : _____
4. clarinet : woodwind :: xylophone :
   _____

| composition   brass   chord   percussion |

Name/Date _____

## Art and Music: Object/Class 3

Match the word to the correct analogy.
1. symphony : composition :: portrait : ____
2. pianist : musician :: ballerina : ____
3. aria : opera :: lights : ____
4. actors : play :: singers : ____
5. singers : opera :: dancers : ____

   a. ballet      b. opera      c. dancer
   d. painting      e. stage

Name/Date _____

## Art and Music: Part/Whole & Object/Class 4

Fill in the missing letters.
1. tuba : brass :: oboe : w _ _ d _ _ _ ds
2. reed : bassoon :: slide : t _ _ _ b _ _ e
3. brass : band :: strings : o _ _ h _ _ t _ _
4. mouthpiece : trumpet :: bridge : c _ _ _ _
5. Renoir : Impressionist :: Warhol : P _ p

Name/Date _____

## Art and Music: Object/Class 5

Circle the missing word that completes each analogy.

| 1. | script : play :: score : | symphony | story | painting |
|----|--------------------------|----------|-------|----------|
| 2. | perspective : painting :: harmony : | prose | discord | music |
| 3. | counterpoint : music :: texture : | rough | bark | painting |
| 4. | melody : music :: step : | dance | leap | steppe |
| 5. | rest : pausing :: beat : | stopping | acting | beet |

# Analogies Warm-ups:
# Art and Music Analogies: Object/Function & Description

Name/Date _____

## Art and Music: Object/Function & Description 1

Circle the missing word.

1. charcoal : dry :: watercolor :        wetundgawpolbnnuct
2. wax : bind :: water :                 paintwatecolorthincharcoalpencil
3. pigment : mineral :: acrylic :        vintwilloplastichardsoftmediumdraft
4. pencil : draw :: watercolor :         reddryhatchpaintblueorange
5. painting : decoration :: play :       educentertainmentchnninfotosme

---

Name/Date _____

## Art and Music: Object/Function & Description 2

Circle the best choice.
1. model : pose :: crayon :
   color          wax          red
2. gallery : display :: frame :
   enclose        metal        rectangular
3. bronze : casting :: marble :
   limestone      white        carving
4. charcoal : draw :: glue :
   attach         sticky       liquid

---

Name/Date _____

## Art and Music: Object/Function & Description 3

Draw a line to match the word to the analogy.

1. drum : beat :: rattle :            ring
2. string : vibrate :: bell :         words
3. landscape : scene :: portrait :    medium
4. flowers : subject :: watercolor :  person
5. script : story :: lines :          shake

---

Name/Date _____

## Art and Music: Object/Function & Description 4

Fill in the missing letters.
1. painting : picture :: bust :
   _ _ u _ _ t _ _ e
2. play : performance :: paintings :
   e _ _ _ b _ _
3. pencil : draw :: violin : p _ _ _
4. pastel : medium :: mountains :
   _ _ b _ _ _ t

---

Name/Date _____

## Art and Music: Object/Function & Description 5

Unscramble the last word in each analogy. Write the answers on your own paper.
1. person : subject :: acrylics : memdiu
2. brush : paint :: plate : rtinp
3. director : play :: conductor : ynmsphoy
4. set : play :: canvas : intipnag
5. trumpet : metal :: violin : odow

# Analogies Warm-ups:
## Art and Music Analogies: Antonyms, Synonyms, and Homophones

Name/Date _____

_____

### Art and Music: Antonyms, Synonyms, Homophones 1

Circle the best choice to complete each analogy.

1. black : white :: smooth :

   glossy    polished    rough

2. silence : sound :: loud :

   noise    soft    deafening

3. slow : fast :: wet :

   dry    damp    water

4. colorful : gray :: fancy :

   ornate    carved    plain

5. detailed : simplified ::

   foreground :

   background    front    close

Name/Date _____

### Art and Music: Antonyms, Synonyms, Homophones 2

Fill in the correct word from the box for each analogy. Write the answers on your own paper.

1. vertical : horizontal :: narrow :
2. land : sea :: landscape :
3. positive : negative :: background :
4. low : high :: light :

| seascape |
| foreground |
| dark |
| wide |

Name/Date _____

### Art and Music: Antonyms, Synonyms, Homophones 3

Draw a line to match the word to the analogy.

1. smooth : rough :: straight :          beat
2. horizontal : vertical :: thick :      curved
3. band : banned :: base :               thin
4. aisle : isle :: beet :                bass

Name/Date _____

### Art and Music: Antonyms, Synonyms, Homophones 4

Fill in the missing letters.

1. choral : coral :: hew : _ _ e
2. color : hue :: light : p _ _ e
3. crimson : red :: ultramarine : b _ _ _
4. emerald : green :: golden : y _ _ _ _ w

Name/Date _____

### Art and Music: Antonyms, Synonyms, Homophones 5

Unscramble the last word in each analogy.

1. fast : slow :: short : nogl _____
2. solo : alone :: duet : prai _____
3. theme : idea :: variation : cnehag _____
4. inversion : reverse :: tempo : sedpe _____

# Analogies Warm-ups:
# Math Analogies: Sequence and Number

---

Name/Date _____

## Math: Sequence and Number 1

Circle the best choice.

1. first : second :: third :
   three   fourth   ordinal

2. one : two :: six :
   seven   cardinal   sixth

3. A : B :: C :      letter   fourth   D

4. one : first :: two :
   cardinal   second   three

5. 4 : four :: 9 :   ninth   nine   numeral

---

Name/Date _____

## Math: Sequence and Number 2

Draw a line to match each word to the correct analogy.

| 1. | tenth : ten :: hundredth : | 10,000 |
| 2. | 120 : 121 :: 130 : | million |
| 3. | 1,000 : 1,001 :: 10,000 : | 131 |
| 4. | 999 : 1,000 :: 9,999 : | hundred |
| 5. | 1,000 : thousand :: 1,000,000 : | 10,001 |

---

Name/Date _____

## Math: Sequence and Number 3

Underline the correct number

1. 5 : fifth :: 7 :            seveneightseventhnine

2. fifth : fourth :: third :    fourththreesecondthree

3. 1 : first :: 6 :            sixthsixnumeralfifthfour

4. eleven : thirteen :: fifteen :    fourteensixteenseventeenfifteenth

5. 10 : ten :: 20 :            twenty-onethirtytwentyfortyfiftytwelve

---

Name/Date _____

## Math: Sequence and Number 4

Fill in the missing letters.

1. 100 : hundred :: 100,000 :
   h _ _ d _ _ d   th _ _ s _ _ d

2. 99 : hundred :: 999,999 : m _ _ _ _ _ n

3. 29 : thirty :: 999 : t _ _ _ _ _ d

4. 70 : eighty :: 90 : h _ _ d _ _ d

5. 59 : sixty :: 89 : _ _ n_ t _

---

Name/Date _____

## Math: Sequence and Number 5

Complete each analogy with the next item in the sequence or the correct relationship.

1. 11 : 12 :: 100,000 : _____

2. 15 : 150 :: 150 : _____

3. one : ten :: ten : _____

4. 1,000,000 : million :: 1,000,000,000 :
   _____

5. abcde : edcba :: vwxyz : _____

---

# Analogies Warm-ups:
# Math Analogies: Pattern

---

Name/Date _____

## Math: Pattern 1

Circle the best choice.

1. ABA : BAB :: BCB :   CBC     BBC     CCB
2. ddb : bbd :: cca :     caa     aca     aac
3. BbB : CcC :: DdD :    EEE     eee     EeE

4. fff : ggg :: lll :        nnn     eee     mmm
5. XOX : xox :: OXO :    OOO    oxo     xxx

---

Name/Date _____

## Math: Pattern 2

Fill in each analogy with the correct term from the box.

| ggGG |
| hIjK |
| RrrR |
| D |
| 8, 88 |

1. 1A : 2B :: 3C : 4_____
2. 1, 11 : 2, 22 :: 7, 77 : _____
3. aaAA : ccCC :: eeEE : _____

4. aBcD : bCdE :: gHiJ : _____
5. MmmM : NnnN :: QqqQ : _____

---

Name/Date _____

## Math: Pattern 3

Match each term to the correct analogy.

1. 1A1A : 2A2A :: 5A5A : ____
2. 1010 : 100100 :: 10001000 : ____
3. 11aa : 22bb :: 77gg : ____

4. #$ : #$# :: ##$$ : ____
5. I : II :: X : ____

a. 88hh
b. ##$$##
c. XX
d. 1000010000
e. 6A6A

---

Name/Date _____

## Math: Pattern 4

Fill in the missing letters.

1. 2, 4, 6, 8 : even :: 1, 3, 5, 7 : o _ _
2. 5, 10, 15 : fives :: 10, 20, 30 : t _ _ _
3. 1, 2, 3 : cardinal :: first, second, third : _ r _ _ _ al

4. 1, 2, 3 : natural :: -1, 0, 1 : _ n _ _ _ er
5. 1, 2, 3 : natural :: 1/2, 1/4, 1/8 : _ a _ _ _ n _ l

---

Name/Date _____

## Math: Pattern 5

Circle the best match to complete each analogy.

1. 3, 6, 9, 12 : multiples of 3 :: 6, 12, 18, 24 :   multiples of 6   multiples of 2
2. 1, 4, 7, 10 : plus three :: 1, 6, 11, 16 :    plus two   plus five   plus ten
3. 0.1, 0.2, 0.3 : 1/10, 2/10, 3/10 :: 1, 2, 3 :   10/10, 20/10, 30/10      1/4, 2/4, 3/4

---

# Analogies Warm-ups: Math Analogies: Geometry

Name/Date _____

## Math: Geometry 1

On your own paper, write the following analogies in words. (Example: rectangle : cylinder :: triangle : cone is written as "rectangle is to cylinder as triangle is to cone")

1. acute : obtuse :: less : more
2. square : cube :: triangle : pyramid
3. triangle : cone :: circle : sphere
4. rectangle : rectangular prism :: triangle : triangular prism

Name/Date _____

## Math: Geometry 2

Draw a line to match the word to the correct analogy.

1. arc : circle :: line segment :           square
2. perimeter : rectangle :: circumference :   parallel
3. congruent : equal :: equidistant :        line
4. quadrilateral : trapezoid :: parallelogram :   circle
5. parallelogram : rhombus :: rhombus :      rectangle

Name/Date _____

## Math: Geometry 3

Fill in the missing letters to complete each analogy.

1. isosceles : equilateral :: rectangle : sq _ _ _ e
2. acute : equilateral :: obtuse : sc _ _ _ ne
3. obtuse angle : parallelogram :: right angle :
   r _ _ t _ _ _ le
4. polygon : closed curve :: square : q _ _ _ ri _ _ t _ _ a _

Name/Date _____

## Math: Geometry 4

Unscramble the last word in each analogy.

1. vertex : angle :: end point : ayr _____
2. 1 end point : ray :: 2 end points : neli smteneg
   _____
3. segment : limited :: line : snesdle _____
4. inside : outside :: interior : tereioxr _____

Name/Date _____

_____

## Math: Geometry 5

Circle the best choice.

1. four : square :: three :
   hexagon
   equilateral triangle
   rectangle
2. hexagon : shape :: five :
   six
   number
   half
3. protractor : angle :: ruler :
   line segment
   measure
   count
4. triangle : three :: pentagon :
   ninth
   building
   five
5. seven : heptagon :: eight :
   quadrangle
   octagon
   triangle

# Analogies Warm-ups:
# Math Analogies: Measurement

---

Name/Date _____

## Math: Measurement 1

Circle each missing word.

1. inch : foot :: foot :     yard     inch   mile
2. foot : yard :: yard :     mile     inch   yard
3. cup : pint :: pint :      cup      quart  gallon
4. pint : quart :: quart : gallon  quart  pint
5. inch : standard :: paperclip :
   nonstandard   inch   gram

---

Name/Date _____

## Math: Measurement 2

Complete the analogy with a word from the box.

1. five : number :: inch : _____
2. inch : length :: ounce : _____
3. second : minute :: minute : _____
4. minute : hour :: hour : _____
5. hour : day :: day : _____

| day weight month hour unit |

---

Name/Date _____

## Math: Measurement 3

Draw a line to match the word to the analogy.

1. year : time :: ton :                    liter
2. degree : temperature :: mile :   kilogram
3. mile : kilometer :: gallon :         centimeter
4. ounce : gram :: inch :               distance
5. meter : kilometer :: gram :        weight

---

Name/Date _____

## Math: Measurement 4

Fill in the missing letters.

1. C : Celsius :: F : F _ hr _ _ h _ i _
2. m : meter :: km : ki _ _ _ e _ _ r
3. mm : millimeter :: cm : c _ _ ti _ _ t _ r
4. kg : kilogram :: g : g _ _ m
5. mm : millimeter ::
   mg : m _ _ _ i _ _ a _

---

Name/Date _____

## Math: Measurement 5

Read each analogy and then write it in analogy notation using colons.

1. L is to liter as mL is to milliliter _____

2. centi is to hundredth as milli is to thousandth _____

3. Celcius is to temperature as gram is to weight _____

4. meter is to length as liter is to volume _____

5. staple is to millimeter as highway is to kilometer _____

# Analogies Warm-ups:
# Math Analogies: Fractions

---

Name/Date _____

## Math: Fractions 1

Circle the best choice to complete each analogy.

1. 1/5 : fifth :: 1/6 :        six        seventh    sixth

2. third : 1/3 :: half :        1/4        1/2        0.25

3. 1/4 : fourth :: 1/7 :        seventh    eighth     seven

4. 1/8 : 1/9 :: eighth :        nine       eight      ninth

5. 10 : 1/10 :: ten :        eleventh   0.01       tenth

---

Name/Date _____

## Math: Fractions 2

Finish each analogy with a term from the box.

1. 0.5 : 1/2 :: 0.2 : _____

2. 0.2 : two-tenths :: 0.3 : _____

3. 0.2 : 0.02 :: tenths : _____

4. 0.02 : 0.002 :: hundredths : _____

5. 0.25 : quarter :: 0.5 : _____

> **hundredths  thousandths  half  1/5**
> **three-tenths**

---

Name/Date _____

## Math: Fractions 3

Draw a line to match the term to the analogy.

1. 5/10 : half :: 10/10 :        0.25

2. 3/3 : whole :: 1/3 :        third

3. 2/4 : 0.5 :: 1/4 :        quarter

4. 3/6 : 1/2 :: 3/12 :        1/4

5. 1/2 : half :: 1/4 :        whole

---

Name/Date _____

## Math: Fractions 4

Fill in the missing letters.

1. 3/9 : third :: 2/10 : f _ _ _ h

2. 2/12 : sixth :: 3/21 : s _ _ _ _ th

3. 10/70 : seventh :: 10/30 : t _ _ _ d

4. 0.70 : seven-tenths :: 0.90 :

   n _ _ e-t _ _ _ h _

5. 0.8 : tenths :: 0.008 : th _ _ s _ _ d _ _ s

---

Name/Date _____

## Math: Fractions 5

Underline the best choice to complete each analogy.

1. 0.7 : 7/10 :: 0.07 :        7     7/10    7/100

2. 7/9 : 14/18 :: 5/6 :        10/12    20/25    15/30

3. 12/15 : 4/5 :: 6/9 :        1/2    4/5    2/3

4. 0.17 : 17/100 :: 0.017 :        17/10    17/1,000

5. 3/4 : 15/20 :: 7/8 :        22/44    34/98    35/40

# Answer Keys

## Solving Analogies: Related Pairs (pg. 2)
Set 1  1. antonyms  2. part/whole
       3. sequence (order)  4. cause/effect
       5. object/action
Set 2  1. c  2. a  3. d  4. e  5. b
Set 3  1. teaching  2. marker  3. mark
       4. tiny  5. school
Set 4  1. laugh  2. sentence  3. acting
       4. sixth  5. fry
Set 5  1. thin  2. huge  3. two
       4. wall  5. reptile

## Vocabulary Analogies: Object/Characteristic (pg. 3)
Set 1  1. purple  2. yellow
       3. orange  4. red
Set 2  1. thorny  2. opaque  3. hard
       4. smooth  5. heavy
Set 3  1. cool  2. hot  3. shiny
       4. crisp  5. light
Set 4  1. liquid  2. cold  3. strong
       4. cool  5. hot
Set 5  1. e  2. d  3. b  4. a  5. c

## Vocabulary Analogies: Member/Group (pg. 4)
Set 1  1. faculty  2. crowd  3. galaxy
       4. pack  5. crew
Set 2  1. collection  2. senate  3. colony
       4. audience  5. team
Set 3  1. c  2. a  3. e  4. d  5. b
Set 4  1. tree is to grove as flower is to bed
       2. actor is to cast as singer is to chorus
       3. chapter is to book as room is to building
       4. block is to neighborhood as neighborhood is to city
Set 5  1. band  2. team  3. library
       4. herd  5. vineyard

## Vocabulary Analogies: Object/Action (pg. 5)
Set 1  1. sniff  2. flow  3. fly
       4. creak  5. pelt
Set 2  1. bounce  2. sink  3. spray
       4. swim  5. honk
Set 3  1. croak  2. neigh  3. waddle
       4. honk  5. pierce
Set 4  1. bounce  2. roll  3. hop
       4. bound  5. fall
Set 5  1. watch  2. toot  3. rumble
       4. stir  5. break

## Vocabulary Analogies: Part/Whole (pg. 6)
Set 1  1. knife  2. tire  3. belt
       4. watch  5. guitar
Set 2  1. compass  2. music  3. branch
       4. roof  5. cabinet
Set 3  1. e  2. d  3. b  4. c  5. a
Set 4  1. library  2. mouth  3. stadium
       4. glove  5. box

Set 5  1. frame is to picture as fence is to yard
       2. knob is to drawer as handle is to door
       3. piece is to puzzle as letter is to word
       4. mattress is to bed as burner is to stove
       5. inch is to foot as foot is to mile

## Vocabulary Analogies: Object/Purpose (pg. 7)
Set 1  1. contain  2. wear  3. hold
       4. smell  5. hear
Set 2  1. sew  2. smooth  3. print
       4. clean  5. add
Set 3  1. T  2. F  3. F  4. T  5. T
Set 4  1. wash  2. drive  3. eat
       4. serve  5. cool
Set 5  1. sleep  2. clean  3. drink
       4. listen  5. dry

## Vocabulary Analogies: Synonyms and Antonyms (pg. 8)
Set 1  1. level  2. grand  3. glad
       4. declare  5. stop
Set 2  1. dislike  2. work  3. woman
       4. mother  5. take
Set 3  1. restore  2. site  3. country
       4. loyal  5. winner
Set 4  1. depressed  2. laugh  3. like
       4. take  5. colorless
Set 5  1. near  2. grow  3. mistake
       4. verse  5. little

## Vocabulary Analogies: Homophones (pg. 9)
Set 1  1. one  2. bear  3. red
       4. bread  5. piece
Set 2  1. passed  2. hair  3. claws
       4. site  5. nose
Set 3  1. oar is to ore as soar is to sore
       2. here is to hear as herd is to heard
       3. heal is to heel as real is to reel
       4. lead is to led as read is to red
       5. peek is to peak as week is to weak
Set 4  1. mane  2. sale  3. rowed
       4. yule  5. reed
Set 5  1. ant  2. carrot  3. for
       4. not  5. roll

## Vocabulary Analogies: Suffixes (pg. 10)
Set 1  1. perishable  2. worker  3. reader
       4. editor  5. buyer
Set 2  1. strength is to strengthen as length is to lengthen
       2. light is to lighter as dark is to darker
       3. lucky is to luckier as happy is to happier
       4. soft is to softest as hard is to hardest
       5. boy is to boyish as girl is to girlish
Set 3  1. d  2. c  3. e  4. b  5. a
Set 4:  1. citizenship  2. sadness  3. sadly
       4. crying  5. division
Set 5  1. active  2. excitement  3. lifeless
       4. fearful  5. bravery

## Vocabulary Analogies: Prefixes (pg. 11)
Set 1  1. rewrite  2. incomplete  3. disappear
       4. nonprofit
Set 2  1. preheat  2. interstate  3. overspend
       4. misunderstand  5. recopy
Set 3  1. precut  2. repay  3. unsolved
       4. outperform
Set 4  1. submarine  2. semifinals  3. untrue
       4. underground
Set 5  1. impatient  2. imperfect  3. irregular
       4. impossible  5. inattention

## Vocabulary Analogies: Greek and Latin Roots (pg. 12)
Set 1  1. sound  2. three  3. sight
       4. small
Set 2  1. corner  2. shape  3. foot
       4. eat  5. turn
Set 3  1. rider  2. speak  3. corners
       4. broken  5. foot
Set 4  1. death  2. moon  3. in
       4. father  5. out
Set 5  1. stretch  2. give  3. pressure
       4. more

## Vocabulary Analogies: Clipped Words (pg. 13)
Set 1  1. memorandum  2. influenza
       3. veterinarian  4. laboratory
Set 2  1. helicopter  2. teenager  3. fanatic
       4. caravan  5. dormitory
Set 3  1. d  2. c  3. e  4. a  5. b
Set 4  1. automobile  2. stereophonic  3. necktie
       4. doctor  5. omnibus
Set 5  1. graduate  2. hippopotamus  3. submarine
       4. professor  5. cellular

## Vocabulary Analogies: Acronyms (pg. 14)
Set 1  1. memory  2. announced  3. service
       4. apparatus  5. team
Set 2  1. possible  2. union  3. jockey
       4. ship  5. recorder
Set 3  1. d  2. a  3. e  4. b  5. c
Set 4  1. number  2. imaging  3. quotient
       4. service  5. information
Set 5  1. officer  2. intelligence  3. head
       4. video  5. grade

## Vocabulary Analogies: Portmanteau Words (pg. 15)
Set 1  1. blotch  2. splutter  3. emoticon
       4. lunch  5. documentary
Set 2  1. e  2. d  3. a  4. b  5. c
Set 3  1. e  2. c  3. d  4. b  5. a
Set 4  1. commercial  2. comedy  3. language
       4. mash  5. slop
Set 5  1. squiggle is to wiggle as telethon is to marathon
       2. pulsar is to star as bionic is to electronic
       3. stagflation is to inflation as netiquette is to etiquette
       4. swipe is to sweep as splatter is to splash

## Grammar Analogies: Irregular Verb Forms (pg. 16)
Set 1  1. were  2. caught  3. froze
       4. brought  5. got
Set 2  1. had  2. flew  3. drank
       4. cut  5. bit
Set 3  1. ate  2. bled  3. drank
       4. felt  5. broke
Set 4  1. lay  2. said  3. sold
       4. shook
Set 5  1. grew  2. made  3. rose
       4. took  5. meant

## Grammar Analogies: Parts of Speech (pg. 17)
Set 1  1. verb  2. adverb  3. noun
       4. adjective  5. adverb
Set 2  1. well  2. slowly  3. merrily
       4. greedily
Set 3  1. d  2. c  3. e  4. b  5. a
Set 4  1. adverb  2. adjective  3. noun
       4. verb  5. adjective
Set 5  1. lazily  2. nicely  3. needlessly
       4. internally  5. delightfully

## Phonics Analogies: Long and Short Vowels (pg. 18)
Set 1  1. can  2. fare  3. tape
       4. made  5. fade
Set 2  1. pane  2. plane  3. rate
       4. stare  5. bite
Set 3  1. ride  2. slime  3. prime
       4. spine  5. pine
Set 4  1. gripe  2. site  3. globe
       4. slope  5. tote
Set 5  1. hug is to huge as cut is to cute
       2. slat is to slate as scrap is to scrape
       3. gap is to gape as tap is to tape
       4. ton is to tone as mop is to mope
       5. spit is to spite as fir is to fire

## Phonics Analogies: Blends and Digraphs (pg. 19)
Set 1  1. trend  2. trip  3. fly
       4. glob  5. shore
Set 2  1. snap  2. then  3. trail
       4. shop  5. score
Set 3  1. slid  2. smash  3. plot
       4. knob  5. gray
Set 4  1. land  2. mast  3. bath
       4. wing  5. west
Set 5  1. sl  2. sh  3. sp  4. tr  5. ng

## Literature Analogies: Poetic Devices (pg. 20)
Set 1  1. horse is to neigh as dog is to bow-wow
       2. pig is to oink as duck is to quack
       3. frog is to ribbit as cat is to meow
       4. cow is to moo as sheep is to baa
       5. donkey is to heehaw as chicken is to cluck
Set 2  1. e  2. a  3. d  4. b  5. c
Set 3  1. brrrrrh  2. ding  3. chug
       4. shhh  5. yuck

## Literature Analogies: Poetic Devices (cont.) (pg. 20)
Set 4   1. row          2. budge        3. row
        4. mound        5. truck
Set 5   1. pet          2. dad          3. rag
        4. end          5. poem

## Literature Analogies: Narrative Elements (pg. 21)
Set 1   1. setting      2. conflict     3. character
        4. resolution   5. problem
Set 2   1. setting      2. resolution   3. poverty
        4. problem
Set 3   1. d    2. e    3. a    4. c    5. b
Set 4   1. resolution   2. genre        3. conflict
        4. setting      5. character
Set 5   1. setting      2. resolution   3. theme
        4. genre

## Literature Analogies: Parts of a Book (pg. 22)
Set 1   1. book         2. paragraph    3. index
        4. contents     5. beginning
Set 2   1. after        2. subheading   3. book
        4. glossary
Set 3   1. atlas        2. book         3. caption
        4. encyclopedia 5. almanac
Set 4   1. nonfiction   2. fiction      3. dictionary
        4. diagram      5. globe
Set 5   1. index        2. keyword      3. fiction
        4. sources

## Science Analogies: Sequence (pg. 23)
Set 1   1. sandstone    2. slate        3. tuff
        4. fossil
Set 2   1. seed is to sprout as sprout is to stem
        2. pollen is to seed as seed is to sprout
        3. leaf is to bud as bud is to flower
        4. light is to photosynthesis as photosynthesis is to food
        5. bud is to flower as flower is to fruit
Set 3   1. d    2. e    3. b    4. c    5. a
Set 4   1. sunset       2. new          3. full
        4. dawn         5. spring
Set 5   1. heat         2. herbivore    3. hawk
        4. moth         5. carnivore

## Science Analogies: Part/Whole (pg. 24)
Set 1   1. snake        2. deer         3. eagle
        4. tortoise     5. trunk
Set 2   1. oak          2. fir          3. alligator
        4. lobster      5. cell
Set 3   1. ray          2. deer         3. walrus
        4. leopard      5. snake
Set 4   1. hurricane    2. pulley       3. tree
        4. plant        5. bird
Set 5   1. plant        2. planet       3. crystal
        4. forest       5. walrus

## Science Analogies: Greek and Latin Roots (pg. 25)
Set 1   1. earth        2. animals      3. plants
        4. stars        5. weather
Set 2   1. spectroscope 2. sight        3. make
        4. mind         5. nonliving
Set 3   1. intergalactic 2. lunar       3. sun
        4. sky          5. sail
Set 4   1. air          2. earth        3. life
        4. ocean
Set 5   1. chronometer is to time as thermometer is to heat
        2. photograph is to mark as photosynthesis is to make
        3. cycle is to circle as phobia is to fear
        4. geology is to earth as hydrology is to water
        5. opitcal is to eye as audible is to ear

## Science Analogies: Object/Class (pg. 26)
Set 1   1. metamorphic  2. flower       3. compound
        4. bivalve
Set 2   1. e    2. c    3. d    4. a    5. b
Set 3   1. feline       2. canine       3. carnivore
        4. amphibian    5. wild
Set 4   1. fish         2. reptile      3. living
        4. plant        5. fungus
Set 5   1. storm        2. machine      3. solid
        4. invertebrate                 5. endoskeleton

## Geography Analogies: Part/Whole (pg. 27)
Set 1   1. lake         2. state        3. country
        4. hemisphere   5. river
Set 2   1. e    2. b    3. d    4. a    5. c
Set 3   1. desert       2. river        3. volcano
        4. hydrosphere
Set 4   1. weather      2. survey       3. desert
        4. plateau
Set 5   1. neighborhood 2. town         3. country
        4. mountains    5. city

## Geography Analogies: Object/Class (pg. 28)
Set 1   1. Maui is to island as Everest is to mountain
        2. Pacific is to ocean as Baja is to peninsula
        3. Africa is to continent as Hawaii is to island
        4. Mojave is to desert as Atlantic is to ocean
        5. Erie is to lake as Columbia is to river
Set 2   1. ocean        2. river        3. desert
        4. nation       5. bay
Set 3   1. e    2. b    3. d    4. a    5. c
Set 4   1. sea          2. river        3. nation
        4. continent    5. city
Set 5   1. nation       2. language     3. mountains
        4. longitude    5. river

## Geography Analogies: Object/Place (pg. 29)
Set 1   1. Arizona      2. Paris        3. California
        4. Naples
Set 2   1. b/e   2. c   3. a   4. b/e   5. d
Set 3   1. Capistrano   2. Rome         3. New York
        4. Hawaii       5. Eygpt

## Geography Analogies: Object/Place (cont.) (pg. 29)

Set 4   1. city         2. land         3. state
        4. pond         5. mountains
Set 5   1. ocean        2. mountains    3. country
        4. stream       5. Africa

## Geography Analogies: Object/Description (pg. 30)

Set 1   1. decade       2. long         3. carved
        4. eroded       5. agricultural
Set 2   1. Arctic is to cold as Sahara is to hot
        2. metropolis is to large as village is to small
        3. rain forest is to wet as desert is to dry
        4. plains are to flat as mountains are to steep
Set 3   1. large        2. small        3. rolling
        4. velvety
Set 4   1. public       2. peak         3. wide
        4. steep        5. high
Set 5   1. warm         2. barren       3. low
        4. draining

## Health Analogies: Part/Whole & Object/Class (pg. 31)

Set 1   1. hand         2. leg          3. backbone
        4. nose         5. skull
Set 2   1. arm          2. foot         3. torso
        4. leg          5. tooth
Set 3   1. lung         2. ear          3. skeleton
        4. chest        5. arms
Set 4   1. nutrition    2. protein      3. grains
        4. dairy        5. vegetable
Set 5   1. fat          2. fitness      3. fiber
        4. fruit        5. dairy

## Health Analogies: Object/Function & Object/Description (pg. 32)

Set 1   1. digest       2. dissolve     3. deliver
        4. bend
Set 2   1. e    2. c    3. a    4. d    5. b
Set 3   1. stand        2. pump         3. collect
        4. control      5. pipe
Set 4   1. cool         2. balance      3. fitness
        4  eat          5. read
Set 5   1. fattening    2. slow         3. wooden
        4. active       5. disinfect

## Health Analogies: Various Skills (pg. 33)

Set 1   1. outside      2. weak         3. spectator
        4. tired
Set 2   1. big          2. chart        3. mind
        4. thoughts     5. eye
Set 3   1. heard        2. hoarse       3. activity
        4. feat         5. fowl
Set 4   1. sight        2. hazardous    3. harmful
        4. sore
Set 5   1. bend         2. system       3. heard
        4. breathing    5. meeting

## Art and Music Analogies: Part/Whole & Object/Class (pg. 34)

Set 1   1. piano        2. violin       3. band
        4. orchestra
Set 2   1. chord        2. composition  3. brass
        4. percussion
Set 3   1. d    2. c    3. e    4. b    5. a
Set 4   1. woodwinds    2. trombone     3. orchestra
        4. cello        5. Pop
Set 5   1. symphony     2. music        3. painting
        4. dance        5. acting

## Art and Music Analogies: Object/Function & Description (pg. 35)

Set 1   1. wet          2. thin         3. plastic
        4. paint        5. entertainment
Set 2   1. color        2. enclose      3. carving
        4. attach
Set 3   1. shake        2. ring         3. person
        4. medium       5. words
Set 4   1. sculpture    2. exhibit      3. play
        4. subject
Set 5   1. medium       2. print        3. symphony
        4. painting     5. wood

## Art and Music Analogies: Antonyms, Synonyms, and Homophones (pg. 36)

Set 1   1. rough        2. soft         3. dry
        4. plain        5. background
Set 2   1. wide         2. seascape     3. foreground
        4. dark
Set 3   1. curved       2. thin         3. bass
        4. beat
Set 4   1. hue          2. pale         3. blue
        4. yellow
Set 5   1. long         2. pair         3. change
        4. speed

## Math Analogies: Sequence and Number (pg. 37)

Set 1   1. fourth       2. seven        3. D
        4. second       5. nine
Set 2   1. hundred      2. 131          3. 10,001
        4. 10,000       5. million
Set 3   1. seventh      2. second       3. sixth
        4. seventeen    5. twenty
Set 4   1. hundred thousand             2. million
        3. thousand    4. hundred       5. ninety
Set 5   1. 100,001      2. 1,500         3. hundred
        4. billion      5. zyxwv

## Math Analogies: Pattern (pg. 38)

Set 1   1. CBC          2. aac          3. EeE
        4. mmm          5. oxo
Set 2   1. D            2. 8, 88        3. ggGG
        4. hIjK         5. RrR
Set 3   1. e    2. d    3. a    4. b    5. c
Set 4   1. odd          2. tens         3. ordinal
        4. integer      5. rational
Set 5   1. multiples of 6               2. plus five
        3. 10/10, 20/10, 30/10

## Math Analogies: Geometry (pg. 39)

Set 1  1. acute is to obtuse as less is to more
         2. square is to cube as triangle is to pyramid
         3. triangle is to cone as circle is to sphere
         4  rectangle is to rectangular prism as triangle is to triangular prism

Set 2  1. line         2. circle       3. parallel
         4. rectangle    5. square

Set 3  1. square      2. scalene     3. rectangle
         4. quadrilateral

Set 4  1. ray         2. line segment  3. endless
         4. exterior

Set 5  1. equilateral triangle        2. number
         3. line segment    4. five      5. octagon

## Math Analogies: Measurement (pg. 40)

Set 1  1. yard         2. mile        3. quart
         4. gallon      5. nonstandard

Set 2  1. unit         2. weight     3. hour
         4. day        5. month

Set 3  1. weight      2. distance   3. liter
         4. centimeter   5. kilogram

Set 4  1. Fahrenheit   2. kilometer  3. centimeter
         4. gram       5. milligram

Set 5  1. L : liter :: mL : milliliter
         2. centi : hundredth :: milli : thousandth
         3. Celcius : temperature :: gram : weight
         4. meter : length :: liter : volume
         5. staple : millimeter :: highway : kilometer

## Math Analogies: Fractions (pg. 41)

Set 1  1. sixth        2. 1/2         3. seventh
         4. ninth       5. tenth

Set 2  1. 1/5         2. three-tenths  3. hundredths
         4. thousandths  5. half

Set 3  1. whole       2. third      3. 0.25
         4. 1/4         5. quarter

Set 4  1. fifth        2. seventh    3. third
         4. nine-tenths   5. thousandths

Set 5  1. 7/100      2. 10/12     3. 2/3
         4. 17/1,000   5. 35/40